IMAGES 1 OF Maidenhead

MAIDENHEAD
ADVERTISER

IMAGES OF
Maidenhead

LUKE OVER MBE

The Breedon Books
Publishing Company
Derby

First published in Great Britain by
The Breedon Books Publishing Company Limited
44 Friar Gate, Derby, DE1 1DA.
1997

ISBN 1 85983 092 7

Printed and bound by Butler & Tanner, Frome, Somerset.
Cover printed by Lawrence Allen, Weston-super-Mare, Somerset.
Colour film supplied by RPS of Leicester.

Contents

Introduction

IT IS said that a picture paints a thousand words and this book reflects the results of a century of photographers who have committed their pictures to celluloid and created a record of Maidenhead through the decades.

In common with other newspapers, the Maidenhead Advertiser has built up a collection of images of the town and the people who made it what it is today, while providing a record of well-remembered landscapes which have now disappeared in the path of progress.

Please come with me, dear reader, on a fascinating step back in time which explores the town's varied and colourful past through the images of yesteryear captured on film by our photographers.

Their work provides us with a remarkable pictorial insight which chronicles the life and times of Maidonians and hopefully in some way explains why and how Maidenhead has developed into the town we see today

The paper's photographic archives, whilst extensive, do not survive for the whole period and for this book the gap has been filled from the photographic collection in Maidenhead Library with plates that appeared in the early editions of the Advertiser. For this favour we are extremely grateful to the Berkshire Library Service and the reference staff at Maidenhead.

Acknowledgement should also be made for the valuable contribution of local historian Luke Over in compiling this selection of photographs which hopefully reflect life in Maidenhead over the past 130 years.

I do hope that our book brings back many happy memories for you and as you turn the pages, look carefully, you may well be one of the hundreds of people who are featured in this pictorial record.

Gerald Baylis
Chairman
Maidenhead Advertiser

Early Settlement

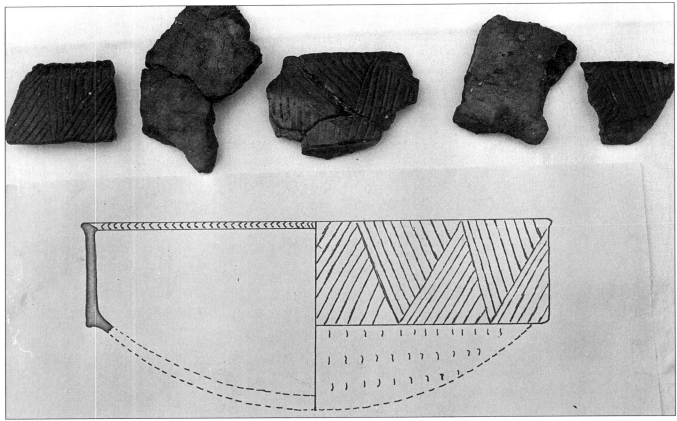

New Stone Age pottery, *c.*2000BC, excavated at Canon Hill, Braywick.

Bronze Age huts being excavated at Weir Bank Stud Farm, Bray, in June 1991.

Local historian James Rutland excavating a Roman villa on Castle Hill in 1886.

Roman excavations at Strand Castle site, Cookham, in 1968.

Excavations on the site of Domesday Maidenhead in 1969.

Archaeologist Luke Over examines finds on the Maidenhead Domesday site dig in 1966.

Excavations in 1972 at Spencers Farm on the Norman manor house associated with the Domesday site of Maidenhead.

An early Medieval well excavated in 1969 at the Domesday manor house.

Industrial hearths of the medieval period excavated at Elentone manor house in 1966.

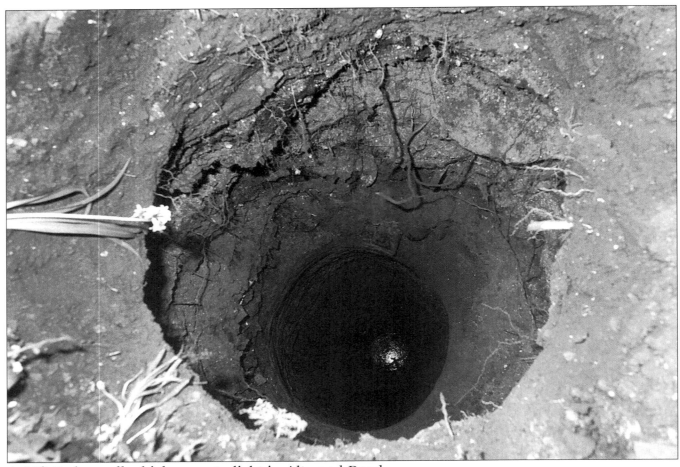

A 90ft Tudor well which came to light in Altwood Road.

Victorian and Edwardian Scenes

The White Hart, the town's largest coaching inn, which stood in the High Street.

Station Approach about 1875 showing the offices of the short-lived *Maidenhead Chronicle*.

Stuchbery's Stores, Maidenhead's first supermarket, in 1880.

Beating the Bounds in 1886 with the Mayor, William Woodbridge, a local builder.

Crowds at Maidenhead Regatta in the 1890s. Many people travelled down from London for this event.

The lower High Street around 1895 with the Swan Inn and the Red Lion coaching inn.

Queen Street in 1895.

The High Street in 1897 during the celebrations for Queen Victoria's Diamond Jubilee.

Mr Nicholson who
started a brewery
in Maidenhead in
Victorian times.

Laying the foundations for the Jubilee Clock in 1899.

The Relief of Mafeking was celebrated in the High Street in May 1900.

High Street and King Street junction in 1900.

The return of local volunteers from the Boer War gathered outside the Guildhall in 1901.

The death of Queen Victoria is announced outside the Guildhall in 1901.

Maidenhead Bridge and the Toll Gates around 1890.

The Toll Gates and Bridge Road *c*.1890.

The Toll Gate at Maidenhead Bridge. Tolls were abolished in 1903.

Celebrations for the coronation of Edward VII in 1901.

The Beating of the Bounds ceremony outside the Maidenhead Workhouse in 1901.

The Two Brewers on Marlow Road and High Street corner in 1904.

Early commuters in Station Approach in 1904.

The top of Maidenhead High Street in 1904.

Bridge Road in the early part of the century.

Edward Biggs' jewellers shop in the High Street in 1905. Biggs were jewellers to the Royal Family and often had royal visitors.

Bridge Road approach to Maidenhead Bridge *c*.1905.

Watkins & Son, Market Street, suppliers of saddles and harness.

The Guildhall, Market Square and High Street in 1906.

Pioneers of the Maidenhead Adult School in 1906.

The Mayor and celebrities at the Royal Counties Show at Maidenhead in May 1907.

A group of Maidonians at the Beating of the Bounds in 1909.

Employees of the Creamery in Queen Street *c.*1908.

The Maidenhead Fire Brigade in 1908.

General Booth of the Salvation Army visits Maidenhead in 1908.

Maidenhead Roller Skating Rink at its opening in 1910.

Another scene of Maidenhead Roller Skating Rink at its opening in 1910.

The bottom of Castle Hill *c.*1910.

Crowds gathered at the top of the High Street for the coronation of King George V in 1911.

Beating the Bounds in 1911.

Proclaiming King George V at Maidenhead in 1911.

The Changing Scene

Maidenhead's temporary cenotaph in the High Street 1919.

Maidenhead High Street looking west about 1920.

The High Street in the 1920s.

Chapel Arches around 1920.

Milk Floats in St Mark's Road in 1920.

The Lower High Street in 1925.

The Bear Hotel and the High Street in the 1950s.

Traffic on Castle Hill in the 1950s.

The Royal Berkshire Regiment in the High Street in 1959.

Shops in Market Street now demolished (1959).

The corner of Queen Street and King Street in the 1960s.

A hive of activity in the High Street of the 1960s.

Demolition in progress in Grove Road.

The first stage of Nicholson's shopping precinct in the 1960s.

High Street and Queen Street corner in 1960.

Maidenhead Market in 1961.

Heatwave queues at Maidenhead Swimming Pool in August 1961.

Demolition in
Market Street in
1961.

The Mayor opens
the automatic
telephone
exchange in 1962.

A fire at Queen Street Post Office in 1961.

Flood relief work in Forelease Road in 1962.

Redevelopment of the Nicholson's Brewery site in 1965.

Aldermaston Atomic marchers in Kidwells Park in 1965.

Mounds of snow on Maidenhead Moor in January 1965.

Edward's forge in Park Street in the 1970s.

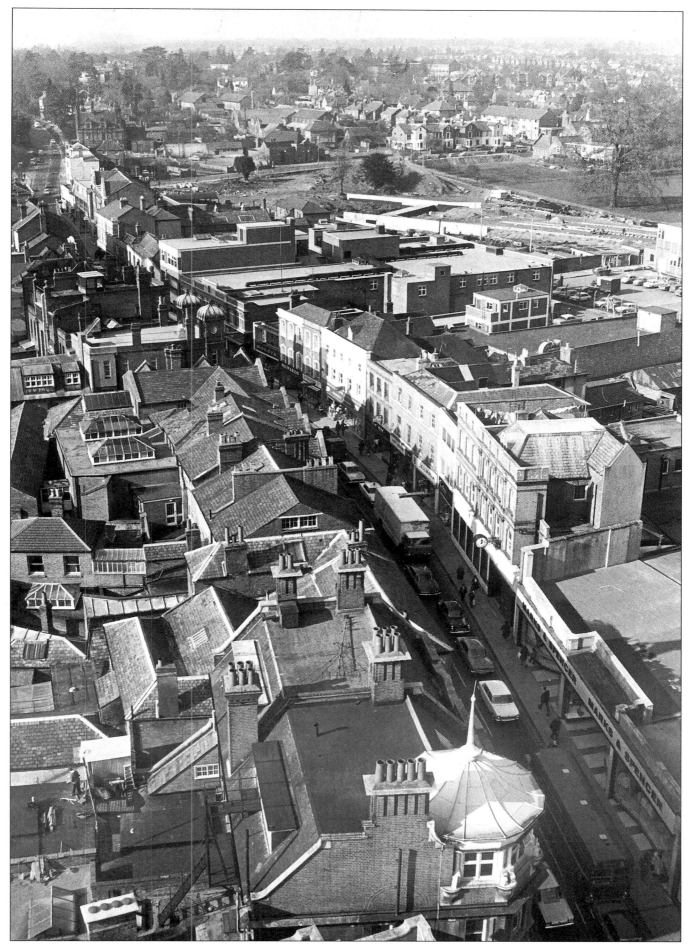

An aerial view of the High Street in 1971 when the relief road was being built.

York Stream which flows through the centre of the town.

King Street and the Jubilee Clock Tower in 1972.

Shops in Market Street 1977.

Mute Swans nesting in the centre of town caused some concern in 1977.

King Street shops demolished to make way for the market *c.*1977.

Chaos at the Railway Station Bridge in 1984.

Lost Landscapes

Langton's Folly, which once stood on the site of the Magnet Leisure Centre. It was built by tramps for John Langton, a local brewer.

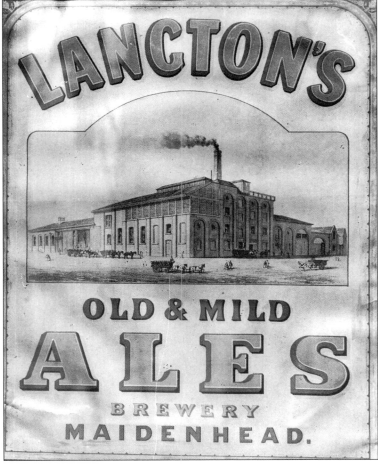

An advertisement for Langton's Brewery, which stood on the corner of Market Street and West Street.

Langton's Brewery building in West Street, now demolished. The firm was founded in the 18th century.

Maidenhead's ABC Cinema, now demolished, which opened in 1928 as the Rialto.

The projection
equipment at the
ABC Cinema, now
demolished.

Maidenhead Bus Station in 1957, with the Coach Station beyond. This area has now been
developed.

Keys or East Berkshire Brewery, now demolished, which stood behind King Street.

St Luke's Cottage Hospital opened in 1879 and demolished in 1978.

The outline of the old Sun coaching inn shows up during demolition in July 1971.

A fire at Fuller's Brewery in Bell Street 1977.

Queen Anne Hotel, Castle Hill, built by J.K.Cooper and displaying all of his brick and tile products, *c.*1970.

Pinkneys Green brickworks.

The Maidenhead Building Society at Tudor House, King Street (1956).

The Cross Keys public house in West Street in 1958.

The Pagoda House in Ray Mill Road West (1962).

A lost landscape. Nicholson's Brewery and Moffatt Street in 1950.

Demolition of the White Hart in the High Street 1965.

Demolition of Nicholson's Brewery in November 1962.

The last resident of Garden Cottages before they were demolished (July 1961).

The back of Garden Cottages in 1961.

Demolition of Garden Cottages in 1962.

The old Carnegie Library in St Ives Road in 1958.

The Plough public house at the bottom of Boyn Hill in 1973.

St Ives House, which stood on the site of the present Town Hall in St Ives Road.

The old Fire Station in Park Street during demolition in the 1930s.

Demolition of St Ives Hotel in 1957.

The old Police Station in the Broadway in 1970.

Demolition of the Guildhall in February 1963.

The demolition of St Paul's Church, Hightown Road, in 1959.

All Saints'
Church,
Braywood, in
1959.

The demolition of All Saints' Church, Braywood,
in 1962.

The Salvation Army citadel in Queen Street in
1974.

Bridge Street Chapel during Harvest Festival in 1905.

The borough church of St Mary's, rebuilt in 1824.

Civic Functions

The opening of Maidenhead's War Memorial by Lord Desborough in 1920.

Lady Astor and dignatories at the opening of Empire Shopping Week, 1928.

Alderman Oldershaw (left) receives the freedom of the town from Mayor Frank and Town Clerk Stanley Platt in the 1940s.

General Montgomery with Mayor L.F.Oldershaw and dignitaries at the ceremony in which he was given the Freedom of the Borough in 1945.

General
Montgomery
inspects the local
troops in 1945.

General Montgomery with all the local mayors at his Freedom Ceremony in 1945.

Mayor Dr O.P.Frank with local aldermen and councillors in 1947.

Mayor J.B.Maudslay and the Maidenhead Borough Council in 1950.

The Guildhall at Maidenhead at the time of Queen Elizabeth II's coronation in 1953. The building was demolished in the 1960s.

The Mayor of Maidenhead's twin town, St Cloud, lays a wreath at the War Memorial (1957).

A group of mayors at the Civic Ball held at Skindles Hotel in 1961.

Alderman H.H.Neve receives the Freedom of the Borough in July 1961.

Laying the foundation stone for the present Town Hall in July 1960.

Building the new Town Hall in 1960.

The Queen and the Duke of Edinburgh at the opening of the Town Hall in June 1962.

The Queen unveils a plaque at Maidenhead Town Hall (June 1962).

Fred Garrett, one-time mace bearer for the Council (1962).

Remembrance Day in 1962.

The Mayoress' chain of office for the Borough of Maidenhead.

A selection of the Borough Plate.

Buildings

The present Public Library in St Ives Road.

St Joseph's Roman Catholic Church before the tower was built.

St Luke's borough church.

The interior of St Luke's Church.

St Mary's borough church in January 1975.

Thames Valley Police Headquarters and Law Courts in Maidenhead.

Harveys the woodworkers in the Arena Building. Here the fuselages for Mosquito aircraft were made during the war.

The interior of the United Reformed Church, built as the Congregational Church in 1785.

The Board Room of the
Maidenhead Union, built in
1896 as part of the Workhouse
complex. This is now part of St
Mark's Hospital.

The Ice House,
Castle Hill. The first
concrete house in
Britain was built
over two Victorian
ice wells.

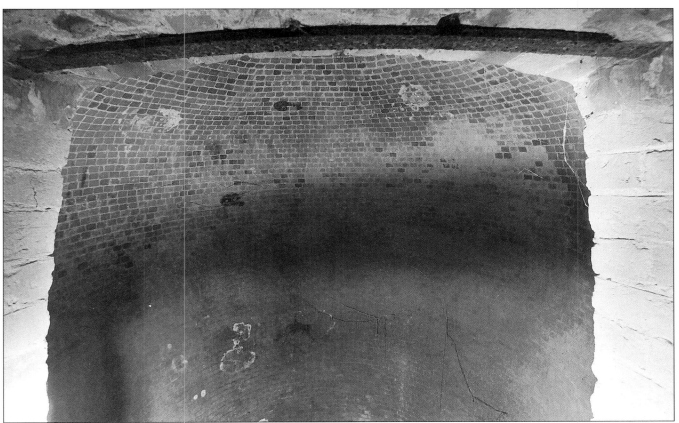

The ice well in the basement of The Ice House, Castle Hill. This belonged to Hamblett, the town fishmonger.

The refurbishment of the Gardener's Arms showing timbers dating to *c.*1580. This is the oldest building in Maidenhead and fronted the Bath Road (1989).

The Windsor Castle public house, Bath Road, so named because the castle could be seen from this viewpoint.

The Bear Hotel, High Street, the last coaching inn to be built, in 1846.

The castle folly on Castle Hill built in 1897 by Hewitt the draper of Maidenhead.

The key to Maidenhead Jubilee Clock Tower presented to Lady Desborough by John Budgen JP on 1 August 1900.

Hazell's greengrocer's shop in Queen Street.

Budgen's shop in the High Street before it became a superstore.

Owen Price's shop on the corner of King Street and Broadway early this century.

Outside Nicholson's Brewery in the High Street in the 1920s.

A fire at Gude's photographic shop on the Colonnade in 1900.

Woodhouse, the family grocer, in Bridge Street.

People and Events

The class of 1905 at the British School, West Street. Most of the boys in the front row died in World War One.

The Pond House Bung Club outing to Brighton by charabanc in June 1922.

Father Christmas in Brock Lane around 1950.

Salute the Soldier Week in Kidwells Park in 1944.

More ceremonials from Salute the Soldier Week in Kidwells Park in 1944.

Mayor J.B. Maudslay at the Clean Food Exhibition in June 1950.

An early production at Maidenhead from Mr Pym's Players.

A performance of *The Merry Wives of Windsor* at Taplow Court in 1962.

Maidenhead Operatic's production of *Princess Ida* at the Guildhall in 1962.

Maidenhead High School production of *The Bartered Bride* in March 1965.

Mr E.Harris wins the Advertiser Cup at Cookham Horticultural Show in 1962.

An ATC Rally at White
Waltham Airfield in 1962.

Timothy Dill Russell,
escapologist, performs at St
Joseph's Fete in 1962.

The College of Art
Fashion Parade in
1962.

The Royal East Berkshire Show at Littlewick in 1962.

A cat show in progress at Pearce Hall in 1962.

Health and beauty classes at Pearce Hall in 1962.

Sorting Christmas mail at Pearce Hall in 1960.

A prize-winning garden in Blenheim Road in July 1961.

Maidenhead's first traffic wardens report for duty.

The Ellington Morris Men in 1978.

A reconstruction of the signing of Maidenhead's Charter of Incorporation by Queen Elizabeth I in 1582, at the 'Maidenhead 400' celebrations with the Mayor, Bert Bellworthy.

The Grimm Players float during the Silver Jubilee carnival in 1977.

Historical Bigheads parade on Littlewick Green during the Queen's Jubilee celebrations in 1977.

The Town Crier at the Cookham Jubilee celebrations in 1977.

Royalty & Celebrities

Edward VII, as the Prince of Wales, takes tea on Monkey Island, Bray about 1908.

The Duchess of Kent visits the town during World War Two.

Princess Marina, Duchess of Kent, takes tea with Alderman Oldershaw in the 1940s.

The Duchess of Kent with members of the WVS at the canteen in St Ives Hotel in 1945.

Princess Alexandra opens the George VI Club for the Elderly in 1957.

Princess Alexandra at Maidenhead High School in June 1959.

The Duke of Edinburgh watches a weighing demonstration at Grasslands Research at Hurley in 1958.

Prince Charles with Mayor Kit Aston on his appointment as High Steward in 1975.

The Queen and Mayor Kit Aston land at Cookham during the Jubilee celebrations.

Princess Anne cutting the cake at WAMSDAD HQ in Braywick Road.

Princess Diana visits the Pine Lodge Hospice.

Lady Astor of Cliveden, Britain's first woman Member of Parliament.

Lady Astor and Mr H.R.Neate examine a rubber duck for the hydrotherapy pool at Cliveden Hospital (1956).

Lady Nancy Astor opens new gates at Cliveden in 1959.

Lord and Lady Attlee at Bisham School Fete in July 1962.

Norman Wisdom causes chaos in Wooburn signal box in 1958.

Norman Vaughan opens the Plaza Bingo Hall in October 1962.

Tommy Steele plays charity football at Maidenhead in 1962.

Ralph Reader and the Boy Scout's *Gang Show* at the Town Hall in April 1965.

Dirk Bogarde with a film production company in St Ives Road in 1963.

Transport and Highways

A coach stop at Skindles Hotel at the turn of the century.

Jonathan Clarke, drayman for Nicholson's Brewery.

Mr Timberlake and his velocipede in 1962.

Taxi cabs in Station Approach about 1920.

Mayor Robinson inspects a GWK car manufactured in Maidenhead *c*.1984.

A crashed car at Hewen's Garage in 1962.

Maidenhead Fire Brigade
appliance in 1962.

The Maidenhead
Bypass under
construction at
Thicket
Roundabout.

Maidenhead Bypass in 1959: construction at Cox Green.

Maidenhead Bypass 1959: the railway bridge at Cox Green

Maidenhead Bypass 1959: construction of the river bridge at Bray.

The opening of the Maidenhead Bypass in June 1961.

Maidenhead's first bus service which ran from the Bear Hotel to Streatley in 1915.

An open-backed Thames Valley double-decker bus in use in 1940.

Thames Valley Bristol bus number 774 in Maidenhead Coach Station in 1957. This lightweight vehicle was designed to cross Marlow suspension bridge.

The Maidenhead Riverside bus crossing Cookham Bridge in 1960.

Maidenhead Riverside Station in 1871. It was demolished in the same year.

A silver trowel presented by the builder of Maidenhead Station to the Mayor on 3 May 1871.

Brunel's railway bridge and the sounding arch from the towpath, pictured in 1904.

The workforce associated with the widening of the Brunel railway bridge across the Thames in 1893.

The destruction of Cherry Garden Lane railway bridge during the widening of the Great Western Railway in 1892.

A soldier guards one of Brunel's railway bridges during World War One.

Maidenhead Railway
Station during the
railway strike of October
1962.

Mr Wheeler and Mr
Manning at Furze
Platt Halt in 1962.

Wellwishers say farewell to the 'Marlow Donkey' train which ran from Maidenhead to Marlow (July 1962).

A steam train at Maidenhead Station during the centenary celebrations of the Maidenhead-Marlow railway in July 1975.

Alderman Cox takes a joyride at the short-lived Maidenhead Aerodrome in 1920.

A demonstration of an inflatable wing aircraft at White Waltham aerodrome in May 1957.

A hanger wrecked by a gale at White Waltham in 1962.

A medical helicopter lands in Kidwells Park in 1962.

The Fairey Rotadyne aircraft designed and built at White Waltham in 1957.

Sporting Maidenhead

Maidenhead United Football Club in 1894-95.

Maidenhead Football Club team of 1911-12.

Maidenhead United win a Cup final against Chesham in April 1965.

Gordon Road School football team 1946.

The Old Maidonians win the Julian Cup in 1962.

St Luke's School football team in 1965.

Members of Maidenhead Cricket Club in 1911.

Maidenhead & Bray Cricket Club XI in 1962.

An early picture of Maidenhead Bowling Club.

A game of bowls in the garden of the Gardener's Arms.

Desborough Bowling Club in its early days.

Desborough Bowling Club v Berks Executive team in May 1958.

The County Bowls finals at Oaken Grove in July 1961.

Awards day for Maidenhead Swimming Club in the 1926 season.

The open-air swimming pool at Maidenhead in the 1950s.

The Real Tennis Club at Holyport in 1961.

The All-Schools swimming gala in July 1961.

The Thames Valley Rugby Club XV in 1963.

Hitcham Boxing Club in action in 1965.

Maidenhead Rowing Club crew in 1962.

Racing at Hawthorne Hill Racecourse in 1961.

River and Floods

River traffic near Boulter's Lock in 1905.

Punters in Boulter's Lock in 1912.

Sunday activity at Boulter's Lock in 1912.

Sixty years later a Sunday afternoon scene at Boulter's Lock in 1972.

Cruising past Bridge House in 1926.

A club outing on a steamer in the 1920s.

Maidenhead Bridge and the Riviera Hotel.

Maidenhead Bridge and Bridge House about 1910.

The frozen river at Maidenhead Bridge in January 1965.

A snowy scene by Maidenhead Bridge.

Skindles Hotel in 1927, before it was rebuilt. It was demolished in 1971.

Skindles Hotel by Maidenhead Bridge as it was in 1972.

The Brigade of Guards Club on the River Thames, now demolished.

The broken-down boathouse on Guards Club Island.

The opening of Guards Club Island to the public.

The Thames Hotel on Ray Mead riverfront *c.*1906.

The Hungaria Club in Bridge Gardens *c.*1927.

The Henry Reitlinger Museum on the River Thames in 1961.

Maidenhead Regatta in 1962.

A boat in collision with Maidenhead Weir in 1962.

The Swan-uppers at Rivergate Cookham in 1962.

Captain John Turk of
Cookham, the Queen's
Swanmaster, at the
Swan Upping in 1981.

Captain Turk and
the Swan-uppers in
Boulter's Lock,
1981.

An early Thames Valley bus travels through the Maidenhead floods around 1930.

Mattingleys express delivery is held up by the Maidenhead flood in the 1950s.

A London-bound coach in the Bridge Street floods of 1947.

The Bridge Street floods of 1947.

The Army helps out during the 1947 floods.

The appropriately named Ark pub in Ray Street during the floods at Maidenhead.

Maidenhead Riverside during the floods of January 1959.

Ray Mill Road West during the 1959 floods.

The floods in Bridge Road in 1959.

Bridge Avenue and Bus Station during the 1959 floods.

A bus in Lower Cookham Road during the floods of 1960.

Round and About

The church of the Holy Trinity, Cookham, which dates to the Saxon period.

The causeway on Cookham Moor in Victorian times.

Cookham High Street with the Bell & The Dragon Hotel in 1959.

Cookham Fire Brigade in 1963.

The Thames lock at Cookham *c.*1885.

The Revd William Scott and his son at Cookham Ferry.

The Toll Gate on Cookham Bridge in 1946.

The abolition of the tolls on Cookham Bridge in August 1947.

Stanley Spencer, the eccentric artist from Cookham, pushing his now famous pram.

Stanley Spencer at his own exhibition in 1958.

The Stanley Spencer Gallery at Cookham, which houses the most important of the artist's paintings. Stanley was born in the village.

The opening of the Stanley Spencer Gallery in April 1962.

St Michael's Church at Bray, built in 1293, as it was in 1904.

The main street of the village of Bray *c.*1895.

Bray village from the church tower in 1972.

The 17th-century Jesus Hospital at Bray *c.*1906.

Shoppenhangers Manor House, built by Thornton Smith during World War One, from ancient glass and timbers.

The moat surrounding the ancient Manor of Foxleys at Bray.

The White Hart, Moneyrow Green, in 1905.

Ockwell's 15th-century manor at Cox Green, Maidenhead.

The Hare & Hounds public house at Braywick.

Holyport Green, Bray, once a market centre, at the turn of the century.

The Eagle pub in Holyport Street, The name was changed to the Belgian Arms after local German prisoners-of-war insisted on saluting it when passing.

Brickmakers and their families at Stud Green, Bray. The brick works, belonging to William Woodbridge, was the main industry in Stud Green until the 1920s.

Oakley Court, Bray. This Gothic mansion was built in 1859 and is now a luxury hotel. When Bray Film Studios were in operation the building featured in many films and was used as Dracula's castle in the film of that name (*c.*1979).

Film set of Paris built at Bray for the film *Isadora*.

A film set in Bray Studios (1965).

Television filming at the Crown Inn at Bray in 1965.

The drive and house of Hall Place, Burchetts Green, which is now the Berkshire Agricultural Institute.

Oxford staging coach outside the East Arms, Hurley (1957).

Shottesbrook Park, home to the Lords of the Manor of Shottesbrook.

The Remembrance Service at Waltham St Lawrence memorial in 1961.

Bisham Abbey on the Thames. The site of three monasteries, this Tudor building is now an important National Sports Centre.

Taplow Court, home of the Earls of Orkney and Lord Desborough. In the foreground is Taplow old churchyard and the Saxon burial mound.

Taplow Court overlooks the Thames and Maidenhead Bridge.

Historical Cliveden House, once the home of the Astors, now an hotel.

The hunt meets outside the Feathers at Cliveden.

Bringing the News — the Maidenhead Advertiser

Mark Taylor (1864-1922), the Town Crier who distributed the news before the *Advertiser* was published.

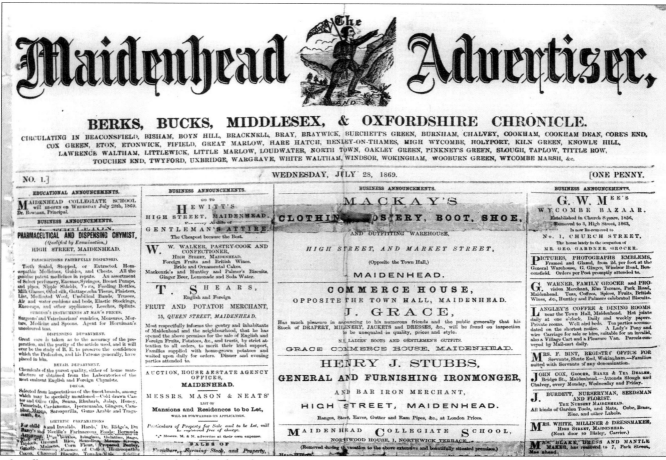

The first copy of the *Maidenhead Advertiser* on 28 July 1869.

The first *Advertiser* office on the corner of Grove Road and Broadway in Victorian times.

Tom Middleton, editor of the *Maidenhead Advertiser* for a long period until 1977.

Queuing for the *Maidenhead Advertiser* in July 1959.

Old style presses at the *Advertiser* printing works about 1960.

Jobbing apprentices at the *Maidenhead Advertiser* in 1961.

Maidenhead Advertiser: Proof correcting (1961).

Maidenhead Advertiser: Setting up type (1961).

Maidenhead Advertiser: Making the machine ready (1961).

Maidenhead Advertiser: View of the composing room (1961).

Maidenhead Advertiser: Working on the stone (1961).

Maidenhead Advertiser: Classified Advertisements (1961).

Maidenhead Advertiser: Scrubbing forms on the press (1961).

Maidenhead Advertiser: Locking up the press (1961).

Maidenhead Advertiser: Packing newspapers (1961).

Maidenhead Advertiser staff in 1965.

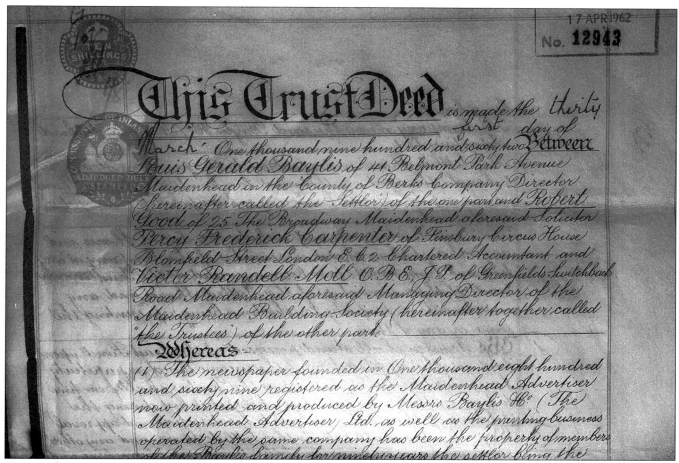

Copy of a Trust Deed for Baylis & Co.

The Baylis & Co stand at the Commonwealth Exhibition at Pearce Hall in May 1961.